Education 4.0 revolution: transformative approaches to language teaching and learning, assessment and campus design

Edited by Kate Borthwick and Alessia Plutino

Published by Research-publishing.net, a not-for-profit association
Contact: info@research-publishing.net

© 2020 by Editors (collective work)
© 2020 by Authors (individual work)

Education 4.0 revolution: transformative approaches to language teaching and learning, assessment and campus design
Edited by Kate Borthwick and Alessia Plutino

Publication date: 2020/08/10

Rights: the whole volume is published under the Attribution-NonCommercial-NoDerivatives International (CC BY-NC-ND) licence; **individual articles may have a different licence**. Under the CC BY-NC-ND licence, the volume is freely available online (https://doi.org/10.14705/rpnet.2020.42.9782490057665) for anybody to read, download, copy, and redistribute provided that the author(s), editorial team, and publisher are properly cited. Commercial use and derivative works are, however, not permitted.

Disclaimer: Research-publishing.net does not take any responsibility for the content of the pages written by the authors of this book. The authors have recognised that the work described was not published before, or that it was not under consideration for publication elsewhere. While the information in this book is believed to be true and accurate on the date of its going to press, neither the editorial team nor the publisher can accept any legal responsibility for any errors or omissions. The publisher makes no warranty, expressed or implied, with respect to the material contained herein. While Research-publishing.net is committed to publishing works of integrity, the words are the authors' alone.

Trademark notice: product or corporate names may be trademarks or registered trademarks, and are used only for identification and explanation without intent to infringe.

Copyrighted material: every effort has been made by the editorial team to trace copyright holders and to obtain their permission for the use of copyrighted material in this book. In the event of errors or omissions, please notify the publisher of any corrections that will need to be incorporated in future editions of this book.

Typeset by Research-publishing.net
Cover illustration: iStock.com/SiberianArt
Cover layout by © 2020 Raphaël Savina (raphael@savina.net)

ISBN13: 978-2-490057-66-5 (Ebook, PDF, colour)
ISBN13: 978-2-490057-67-2 (Ebook, EPUB, colour)
ISBN13: 978-2-490057-65-8 (Paperback - Print on demand, black and white)
Print on demand technology is a high-quality, innovative and ecological printing method; with which the book is never 'out of stock' or 'out of print'.

British Library Cataloguing-in-Publication Data.
A cataloguing record for this book is available from the British Library.

Legal deposit, France: Bibliothèque Nationale de France - Dépôt légal: août 2020.

Table of contents

iv   Notes on contributors

1   Introduction
Kate Borthwick and Alessia Plutino

5   Transforming learning spaces for multilingual interaction: the outcomes of a workshop delivered at the 2020 eLearning Symposium
Cecilia Goria and Lea Guetta

15   Web-based and interactive Italian blended learning course: embedded apps and tools in a structured learning process
Laura Capitani

21   Do blogs as a virtual space foster students' learner autonomy? A case study
Georgie Hannam

29   Integrating MOOCs into traditional UK higher education: lessons learnt from MOOC-blend practitioners
Karla K. de Lima Guedes

37   Task-based language learning through digital storytelling in a blended learning environment
Serpil Meri-Yilan

45   Introducing corpus linguistic tools to EFL undergraduates and trainee teachers
Mária Adorján

53   EAP 4.0: Transforming the English for Academic Purposes Toolkit to meet the evolving needs and expectations of digital students
Andrew Davey and Simone Marx

61   Chinese parents' perceptions and practices of EFL technology usage with young children
Xing Liu

68   Author index

Notes on contributors

Editors

Kate Borthwick is Principal Enterprise Fellow (Educational Innovation) in Modern Languages and Linguistics at the University of Southampton. She leads the University's MOOC programme as Director of Open Online Courses for the University and chairs the University Digital Education Working Group.

Alessia Plutino is Senior Teaching Fellow in Italian at the University of Southampton and also Associate Lecturer of Italian at the Open University. Her areas of interest are on material design, CALL – particularly with regards to student independent learning skills and aspects of cultural and intercultural awareness integrated into language teaching – collaborative learning via social media, and VR. From January 2019, she is conference chair of the e-Learning Symposium, which runs annually at the University of Southampton.

Reviewers

Charlotte Everitt is Senior Teaching Fellow in Modern Languages and Linguistics at the University of Southampton. She teaches e-learning in ELT on the MA ELT/TESOL studies and the MA in applied linguistics for language teaching programmes, and develops and coordinates online and blended courses within the Faculty of Arts and Humanities.

Dr Virginie Pignot-Shahov is Teaching Fellow in French at the Centre for Language Study in Modern Languages and Linguistics at the University of Southampton. She holds a BA in English language and linguistics, a PGCE in modern languages, and a PhD in second language acquisition from the University of Southampton. She is Fellow of the Higher Education Academy.

Laurence Richard is the Director of the Centre for Language Study in Modern Languages and Linguistics at the University of Southampton. After studying English and American civilisation and literature in Bordeaux University, she did a Masters in FLE (français langue étrangère) at La Sorbonne University,

Paris, and did a PGCE at Homerton College, Cambridge. She then completed a Master of Philosophy in second language acquisition at Southampton university.

Author/reviewer

Karla K. de Lima Guedes is Senior Teaching Fellow in the Academic Centre for International Students and a PhD researcher in the Web Science Institute, both at the University of Southampton. Amongst other things, she holds a BA in linguistics and phonetics, an MA in applied linguistics for language teaching, and an MSc in web science.

Authors

Mária Adorján is Senior Lecturer at the English Linguistics Department at Károli Gáspár University, Hungary. She holds a doctoral degree in language pedagogy. Since 2013, she has been a pre-sessional course teacher for the University of Southampton. Her research interests include applied linguistics, curriculum design, and language teaching and learning.

Laura Capitani has many years of experience as teacher of Italian and coordinator at the Maastricht University Language Centre in The Netherlands. Her long-term interest in the use of internet applications and tools for language teaching has led to developing Italian blended-learning language courses for stimulating online students' cooperation and interaction.

Andrew Davey is the Manager of eLanguages Projects and Toolkits at the University of Southampton. He develops e-learning projects, products, and resources, specialising in the creation and usage of learning objects. He is a certified member of the Association for Learning Technology. He comes from a technical background and uses this knowledge to enhance resources whilst retaining a pedagogically-sound approach.

Notes on contributors

Cecilia Goria is Associate Professor in the Department of Modern Languages and Cultures, University of Nottingham. She holds the role of Director of Digital Learning in the Faculty of Arts and is the Academic Leader of the distance learning Master's degree in digital technologies for language teaching. Her areas of interest are the design, principles, and practice of open learning, active learning, and participatory pedagogies in online and blended teaching and learning.

Lea Guetta is Lecturer in Spanish in the Language Centre at the University of Nottingham. She is an experienced language teacher of both Spanish and French. Her teaching experience covers primary, secondary, sixth form, and the higher education sectors. She is also Director of Work-Related Learning in the School of Cultures, Languages, and Area Studies.

Georgie Hannam is a graduate of MA applied linguistics of language teaching at the University of Southampton where she developed her passion for online learning. She now works as a Learning Designer for insendi, where she helps academic institutions build innovative and impactful online courses.

Xing Liu is Lecturer in the College of Foreign Languages and Culture at North Minzu University. Liu has more than 15 years' experience in EFL teaching. She has worked on a variety of EFL issues, including language policy, EFL writing, and SLA.

Simone Marx is the eLanguages Project Assistant at the University of Southampton. She contributes to pre-sessional and in-sessional course design, with a particular focus on the MA in English language teaching and the English for Academic Purposes Toolkit. She completes this work alongside her MA in history at the University of Southampton.

Serpil Meri-Yilan is Assistant Professor at AICU, Turkey. She gained her MA in 2011 and PhD in 2017, in applied linguistics for language teaching at the University of Southampton. She is also currently the research collaborator of ImmerseMe, and senior reviewer for IAFOR Journal of Education. She presents and writes papers on foreign language learning and teaching.

Introduction

Kate Borthwick[1] and Alessia Plutino[2]

Welcome to this collection of short papers from the eLearning Symposium 2020!

The 13th eLearning Symposium was held at the University of Southampton, on the 24th of January 2020. Our theme was 'Education 4.0 revolution: transformative approaches to language teaching and learning, assessment, and campus design'. At the time, the ideas and topics we discussed were future-gazing, but within months, they have become a reality for many of us.

Indeed, as we write this introduction, we have seen the COVID-19 virus sweep the world and lead to dramatic changes in our lives and in how we deliver education. Schools and universities have been forced to embrace digital delivery modes virtually overnight, and students now face an online and/or blended educational experience for many months to come. We ask ourselves: how much of this digital transformation will last? How can we ensure that the lessons we are currently learning about good practice in the use of technology will be developed and maintained beyond this crisis?

Never has the work of our symposium community been more timely, and within this collection you will find help, inspiration, and thought-provoking ideas. This collection represents a small snapshot of the papers, workshops, and other contributions we heard at our 2020 event.

This volume opens with a workshop report dealing with the transformation of physical learning spaces for multilingual interaction. Authors **Cecilia Goria** and

---

1. University of Southampton, Southampton, United Kingdom; k.borthwick@soton.ac.uk; https://orcid.org/0000-0003-2251-7898

2. University of Southampton, Southampton, United Kingdom; a.plutino@soton.ac.uk; https://orcid.org/0000-0001-5552-6753

How to cite: Borthwick, K., & Plutino, A. (2020). Introduction. In K. Borthwick & A. Plutino (Eds), *Education 4.0 revolution: transformative approaches to language teaching and learning, assessment and campus design* (pp. 1-3). Research-publishing.net. https://doi.org/10.14705/rpnet.2020.42.1080

Introduction

Lea Guetta are leading their own transformative project for a Self-Access Centre (SAC) at their university, and they shared their thinking and practical steps so far. Workshop participants discussed the interplay between the innovative use of physical space, the availability of increased amounts of digital content, varied approaches to accessing content, and changing student habits towards how and when to study language. Readers will find the authors' rationale for their SAC redesign, their conclusions, and the summary of the workshop participants' thoughts and feedback illuminating and useful.

Considerations of space, time, and effective education delivery are also evident in the innovative online work presented by **Laura Capitani**. She describes an interactive, blended course in Italian which has been highly effective in mixing self-paced study with focussed online personal learning sessions. Her use of a range of tools and apps has given both students and tutors flexibility over teaching and learning and resulted in a course with a broad appeal to a wide number of diverse learners. **Georgie Hannam** considers space in her chapter: the virtual space offered by blogs. Her case study proposes blogging as a method to encourage learner autonomy and concludes that the tutor's approach and attitude are vital in ensuring such spaces are effective in fostering autonomy.

Every year, the symposium is full of examples of how technology can enrich the experience of students in the classroom. **Karla K. de Lima Guedes** gives an account of her research into the experiences of practitioners who integrate Massive Open Online Courses (MOOCs) into traditional UK higher education teaching. Her chapter finds that educators have a range of reasons for doing this, but often use MOOCs to add an international dimension to their classroom. She gives useful tips for anyone considering blending a MOOC into their learning programme. **Serpil Meri-Yilan** discusses the use of digital storytelling to enrich the task-based language learning experience of her students. She finds that students enjoy the method and it has some effect in improving speaking skills. **Mária Adorján** reports similarly positive results from her students, in relation to the use of corpus linguistic tools with English as a Foreign Language (EFL) undergraduates and trainee teachers. She describes her success in integrating corpus linguistic tools into her programme to enhance linguistic awareness and encourage learner autonomy.

We close with two chapters discussing the importance of attitudes and expectations in technology use for learning. **Andrew Davey** and **Simone Marx** outline the technical changes implemented to a course of online resources in response to evolving learner needs and expectations. These included changes to ensure greater accessibility and inclusivity, structured pathways to guide learning, and an enhanced 'look and feel' for the user experience. Finally, in the last chapter by **Xing Liu**, the focus shifts to the perceptions of parents when trying to understand why learners use apps for EFL learning. She finds that parental beliefs about the importance of language learning in general have an impact on learners' technology use.

We do hope you enjoy this volume of short papers from the eLearning Symposium and that you find inspiration and ideas for your own research and practice. We hope to see you at the symposium in the future, sharing your own work and experience. Keep safe and well.

Acknowledgements

We would like to thank our authors and reviewers for giving their time and expertise to the creation of this volume. Our thanks also go to our symposium attendees and our publishers. Finally, we are grateful to the Confucius Institute in Southampton for sponsoring this publication

1. Transforming learning spaces for multilingual interaction: the outcomes of a workshop delivered at the 2020 eLearning Symposium

Cecilia Goria[1] and Lea Guetta[2]

Abstract

The design of innovative learning spaces currently affects different educational sectors, including university teaching and learning. A parallel can be identified between the weakening of the specialisation of spaces for formal, informal, life-long learning, social interaction, and leisure and the blurring of the boundaries between work/learning and social engagement. Furthermore, a user-centred approach to space design mirrors the ongoing development towards student-centred education, and the emphasis on making these spaces digitally competitive equally reflects the increasing integration of technologies in teaching and learning. This contribution is the report of a workshop delivered at the eLearning Symposium, 24th January 2020, Southampton, which explored possible designs for a learning space conducive to multilingual communication, collaboration, and creativity.

Keywords: space design, language teaching/learning, technology.

---

1. University of Nottingham, Nottingham, United kingdom; cecilia.goria@nottingham.ac.uk; https://orcid.org/0000-0002-4530-4138

2. University of Nottingham, Nottingham, United kingdom; lea.guetta@nottingham.ac.uk

How to cite this chapter: Goria, C., & Guetta, L. (2020). Transforming learning spaces for multilingual interaction: the outcomes of a workshop delivered at the 2020 eLearning Symposium. In K. Borthwick & A. Plutino (Eds), *Education 4.0 revolution: transformative approaches to language teaching and learning, assessment and campus design* (pp. 5-14). Research-publishing.net. https://doi.org/10.14705/rpnet.2020.42.1081

Chapter 1

1. Introduction

This contribution is concerned with the workshop titled 'Transforming learning spaces for multilingual interaction', delivered at the eLearning Symposium, 24th January 2020, Southampton. In this short paper, the content of the workshop is outlined and its outcomes reported.

The workshop focused on the re-design of a physical space that is currently embedded in the Language Centre of the University of Nottingham and specialises in supporting the teaching and learning of modern foreign languages. The purpose of the workshop was to generate innovative design ideas and encourage the participants, predominantly language teachers, to reflect on the design of similar learning spaces in their institutions. The workshop delivery included two distinct sessions; an introduction in which the re-design project and the principles underpinning the practice were outlined, and a hands-on session that engaged the participants in designing learning activities and the related physical spaces.

The space in question, known as the Self Access Centre (SAC), currently functions as a language learning resource centre offering a service to students and staff across the university. The SAC currently hosts language textbooks and dictionaries, magazines and newspapers, and drill-and-practice digital resources accessible through desktop PCs. In terms of furniture, the SAC includes PC booths, bookshelves, one large table, and two areas with low seats with coffee tables.

In December 2018 and 2019, a survey was conducted to gain intelligence on the use of the space. Below is a short summary of the most relevant results:

- 71% of students using the SAC are language specialists;

- 47% use it weekly, 18.6% daily, and 34.3% occasionally; and

- 57.8% use their own devices, 67.6% use the SAC PCs, and 48% use the SAC analogue resources.

2. The SAC re-design project

Prompted by the claims that there is a link between space and learning (Blith & Crook, 2017) and by the notion of built pedagogy (Monahan, 2002) according to which learning is affected by the space within which it takes place, the present state of the SAC is not aligned with current pedagogical trends that place the students at the centre of social constructivist learning experiences. In addition, its emphasis on language-drill resources is contradictory to the communicative language teaching style of teaching practices at Nottingham. Hence, the SAC re-design project was initiated, driven by the wish to transform the existing space into a new flexible, inspiring, future-proofed area to support digitally enhanced, communicative, collaborative, and creative learning and teaching.

A number of considerations have been identified as the drivers for the SAC re-design project. These are:

- learning happens all the time and everywhere; heavily supported by technology and the ease of access to resources that it provides, learning is no longer confined within the walls of classrooms and institutions but takes place at home, at school, at work, and in social places, and at any time;

- the boundaries between work and learning and social engagement are blurred as people become more connected due to social media; and

- the specialisation of spaces for formal, informal, life-long learning, social interaction, and leisure is weakened, reflected in the increasing attention paid to create flexible, and multipurpose spaces, in line with the multitasking nature of 21st century lifestyle.

A degree of inspiration sprang from a visit to the Oodi Central Library in Helsinki, Finland[3]. A public building described as

---

3. https://www.oodihelsinki.fi/en/what-is-oodi

Chapter 1

> "one of the freest buildings in Helsinki, or even the Nordic Countries, where the visitor can do many things and take initiative in what they want to do. It is a constantly learning and developing tool for those living in or visiting Helsinki" (Oodi website[4]).

Through a vibrant and modern space design,

> "Oodi is a meeting place, a house of reading and a diverse urban experience. [It] provides its visitors with knowledge, new skills and stories, and is an easy place to access for learning, relaxation and work" (Oodi website[5]).

While the features of Oodi are not comparable to the scope of the SAC re-design project, it is our aspiration to achieve the vibrancy and social interaction that emerges from Oodi's versatile and inspiring space design.

Other factors that influence our re-design ambitions are:

- the ubiquity of technology heavily impacts teaching and learning practices; and

- teaching and learning practices are increasingly adopted for the implementation of social constructivist pedagogies that put the learners at the centre of the educational experience.

These observations correlate with the principles underpinning JISC's Sticky Campus project, by which

> "[a] sticky campus is a digitally-enabled space where students want to spend time, even when they don't have a formal teaching session to go to. It's a learning environment designed to give students everything

---

4. https://www.oodihelsinki.fi/en/what-is-oodi/architecture/#:~:text=Oodi%20is%20one%20of%20the,living%20in%20or%20visiting%20Helsinki.

5. https://www.oodihelsinki.fi/en/services-and-facilities/

they need for collaborative and solitary study, and to promote active learning. It supports inclusivity and enables rich learning experiences" (JISC, 2019, para 1).

The presence of technology in the relation between learning and spaces finds support in the *pedagogy-space-technology* model (Radcliff, 2009) by which pedagogy, space, and technology are tightly connected and have a reciprocal impact, enhancing, enabling, and extending each other's scopes, functions, and roles (see Figure 1).

Figure 1. Pedagogy-space-technology (Radcliff, 2009, p. 13[6])

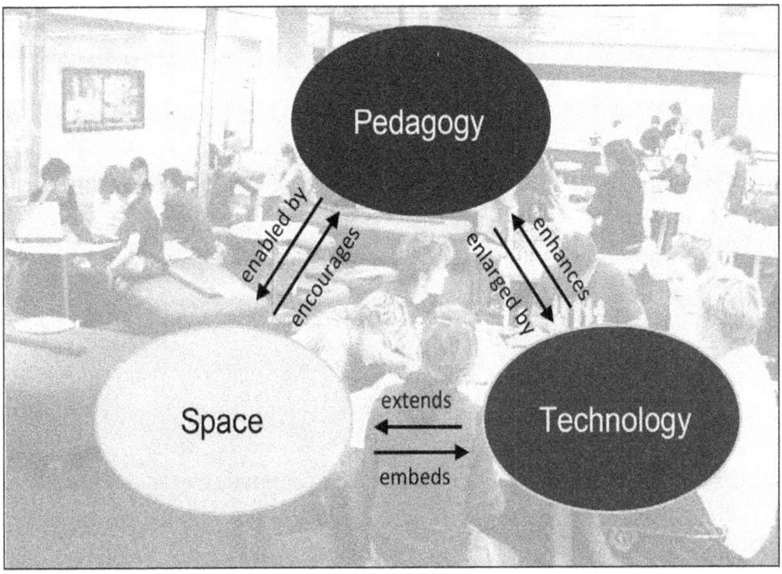

3. Our vision

JISC (2006) states that the individual spaces inside education buildings should be:

---

6. "Support for the original work was provided by the Australian Learning and Teaching Council Ltd, an initiative of the Australian Government Department of Education, Employment and Workplace Relations".

- flexible – to accommodate both current and evolving pedagogies;
- future-proofed – to enable space to be re-allocated and reconfigured;
- bold – to look beyond tried and tested technologies and pedagogies;
- creative – to energise and inspire learners and tutors;
- supportive – to develop the potential of all learners; and
- enterprising – to make each space capable of supporting different purposes (Radcliff, 2009, p. 13).

With this set of principles in mind, the SAC re-design project envisages the shaping of an educational space that:

- invites students to spend time in it, beyond course requirements (cf. Sticky Campus[7]);
- supports interactions in different languages;
- is conducive to collaborative learning and teaching;
- provides students and teachers with the digitally competitive facilities;
- supports creativity especially in media production; and
- is able to cope with different types of activities, ideally happening at the same time, reflecting the multitasking nature of the 21st century lifestyle.

4. Method: one hour workshop

During the workshop, the participants (eight postgraduates and 13 academic staff) were introduced to the thinking behind the SAC re-design project and were asked to engage in activities that elicited ideas as well as reflection on the purposes and shape of learning spaces in the context of language learning and teaching.

The participants were divided into randomly formed groups and the questions were presented one at a time by the authors of this contribution, and intervals of

---

7. http://www.thestickycampus.com/

five to ten minutes were included for the participant to generate their responses. They used flipchart sheets, colour coded post-its, and pen markers to provide and structure their answers. After each question, all groups were given the opportunity to feedback their ideas to the other groups.

The participants were asked to:

- generate ideas for collaborative teaching and learning activities that could take place in the new space;

- identify the technologies that would support those activities;

- think creatively about the type of furniture that best suited the collaborative teaching and learning nature of the new space – for this part of the activity, the participants were asked to draw a floor plan and draw on it their furniture solutions; and

- brainstorm for a catchy name that reflects the purposes of the space.

The outcomes of the workshop are tentatively addressed below.

5. Results and considerations on the outcomes

Responses to the first task, i.e. generating ideas for collaborative teaching and learning activities that could take place in the new space, included:

- poster presentations;
- cultural demonstrations;
- role plays;
- debating;
- language games;
- skill exchange sessions;
- student-led sessions;

Chapter 1

- conversation practice (language café);
- task-based language teaching;
- exhibition space;
- cultural events;
- cinema;
- global issues debate space;
- chill-out zone; and
- virtual reality to learn how to act in different situations and cultures.

Responses to the second task, i.e. identifying the technologies that would support those activities, included:

- whiteboard;
- projector;
- media editing software;
- computers;
- smartphone equipment;
- video/multimedia;
- large screen;
- virtual reality software and hardware; and
- platform to book the space.

Suggestions for suitable furniture (third task) included:

- movable chairs and desks (multidimensional furniture);
- comfortable seating;
- walls that can be moved;
- tables with embedded plugs (computers, multiuse);
- different lights around the room;
- lockers;
- water fountain; and
- multicultural decorations.

Finally, suggestions for a name for the new space included:

- Inspiring Learning Hub;
- Chatty Centre;
- Interactive Learning Lounge;
- Communication Interactive Learning Lounge;
- Open Learning Hub;
- Digital Voice Hub;
- Multilingual Suite;
- e-Media Café;
- Language Exchange Corner; and
- Multilingual Communication Learning Space.

The participants' responses, while in net contrast with the present state of the SAC, given its current emphasis on analogue materials and its focus on individual self-study resources, were highly consistent with the plan of the SAC re-design project to create a flexible and innovative space to foster digitally enhanced, student-centred, collaborative, and communicative language learning and teaching. In particular, the activities suggested in the first task corroborate our need for a space that supports multilingual communication and collaboration, e.g. conversation practice, debating, exhibition space. Furthermore, they support our ongoing transformation towards student-centred education, e.g. presentations, student-led sessions; and highlight the significance of transforming language learning activities into cultural exchanges, e.g. cultural events and global issues debates. They also emphasise the importance of providing opportunities for the development of transferable skills, e.g. skill exchange sessions, task-based language teaching, and of integrating extra-curricular activities, e.g. chill-out zone or cinema in our study programmes.

Similar observations hold for the list of possible names for the new space. These embed features like technology, inspiration, exchange, openness, multilingualism, communication, and social engagement, reflecting the nature of the activities that it would host. Finally, the participants' suggestions for the technology and the furniture to be located in the new space are aligned with the teaching and learning activities proposed and tally with our need to optimise and rationalise educational spaces with multipurpose and flexible solutions.

6. Conclusion

The workshop reported in this paper aimed to elicit reflections on the significance of educational spaces and to generate space design ideas that support communicative and collaborative language teaching and learning.

The workshop provided insights from academics from different institutions, including the input from the eight student participants who added the learners' perspectives to the re-design ideas. The outcomes of the workshop will inform the next phases of the SAC re-design project. In particular, the ideas generated in the workshop will provide supporting external evidence for the project business case and will influence the ideation and realisation of the new space.

References

Blith, B., & Crook, C. (2017). Learning spaces. In E. Duval, M. Sharples & R. Sutherland (Eds), *Technology enhanced learning*. Springer International Publishing AG.

JISC. (2006). Designing spaces for effective learning: a guide to 21st century learning space design. https://webarchive.nationalarchives.gov.uk/20140703004833/http://www.jisc.ac.uk/media/documents/publications/learningspaces.pdf

JISC. (2019, September 10). Sticky campus: the students' verdict. *JISC news*. https://www.jisc.ac.uk/news/sticky-campus-the-students-verdict-10-sep-2019

Monahan, T. (2002). Flexible space & built pedagogy: emerging IT embodiments. *Inventio*, 4(1), 1-19.

Radcliff, D. (2009). A Pedagogy-space-technology (PST) framework for designing and evaluating learning places. In D. Radcliff, H. Wilson, D. Powell & B Tibbetts (Eds), *Learning spaces in higher education: positive outcomes by design* (pp. 9-16). The University of Queensland.

2 Web-based and interactive Italian blended learning course: embedded apps and tools in a structured learning process

Laura Capitani[1]

Abstract

❛ Web-based and Interactive Italian' is a detailed and progressive programme developed by the author for the Maastricht University Language Centre. The course started in 2013, with the intention of catering for the variability in the number of students following the regular courses, as well as broadening the language offer using blended learning. The eight interactive tutor-led Skype sessions are preceded by 80 hours of self-study per level. Starting from a flipped classroom approach, it is structured in three consecutive learning steps. It makes use of existing language apps and tools, like Babbel[2] and Quizlet[3], and of a manual book used at the intermediate levels, as well as bespoke web-based and interactive learning materials as preparation for the oral sessions. The course is still running successfully and represents an effective alternative to traditional courses, offering distance learners the possibility of completing the whole study programme from A1 to B2.

Keywords: web-based, interactive, blended learning, flipped classroom.

---

1. Maastricht University, Maastricht, Netherlands; laura.capitani@maastrichtuniversity.nl

2. http://www.babbel.com

3. http://www.quizlet.com

How to cite this chapter: Capitani, L. (2020). Web-based and interactive Italian blended learning course: embedded apps and tools in a structured learning process. In K. Borthwick & A. Plutino (Eds), *Education 4.0 revolution: transformative approaches to language teaching and learning, assessment and campus design* (pp. 15-20). Research-publishing.net. https://doi.org/10.14705/rpnet.2020.42.1082

1. Introduction

The Maastricht University Language Centre is part of a modern and young university in the South of The Netherlands. The university is well-known for its problem based learning approach. The Language Centre has always aimed to augment the pedagogical value of its courses by using task-based, communicative, online, and web-based approaches. The motivation to learn a less widely used foreign language (such as Italian) can depend on and vary according to several situations (Quan, 2014). One important one is the possibility to physically attend classroom sessions. This might account for a reduced number of participants, which in turn can lead to course cancellation, and ultimately result in courses no longer being made available to students. In this context, in 2013, I developed the web-based and interactive Italian course with the intention of accommodating the decrease in students by using a modern blended learning approach. This web-based and interactive Italian course is still running, and it represents a good alternative to class-based courses. The aim of this paper is to illustrate the course structure and content as well as the success factors of this web-based and interactive way of language learning.

Figure 1. Web-based and interactive Italian: from learning to performing the language

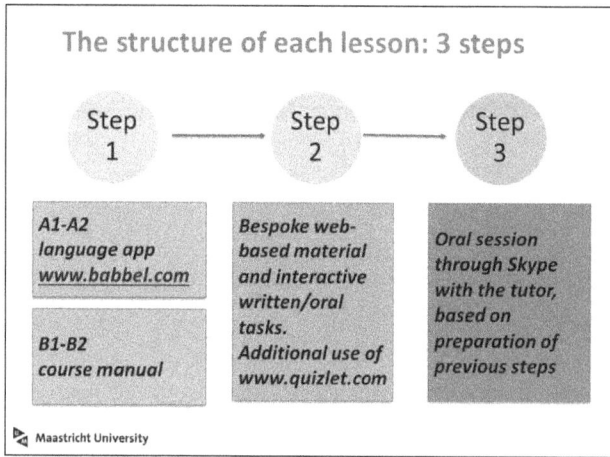

2. Method: starting from existing material on the web

I started by researching what was already on offer in terms of web-based learning. My goal was to find a starting point by identifying tools that already existed which I could use to build a structured course that suited our communicative and task-based approach. In the big universe of apps, tools, and existing language programmes, I found Babbel. This was the only app that assured a good and well-structured base for developing my course, aimed at improving students' oral communication skills. While Babbel was suitable for the goals at beginner levels (A1-A2), a course book was required to meet the needs of intermediate students (B1-B2). I divided the Babbel course and the manual book in eight parts, adding and/or removing parts according to our programme and to the Common European Framework of Reference for languages (CEFR) directives.

2.1. The course in a nutshell

This course offers four language levels (A1 to B2). The students attain each level through eight one-to-one, tutor-led, 30-minutes Skype sessions and a maximum of 80 self-study hours, following a three step learning plan (Figure 1). Aimed at a flipped classroom, task-based approach, this plan is based on existing language apps, a course manual, and additional web-based and interactive additional material. Students following this course must sit the same final exam covering the four language skills, as offered in the traditional 28 contact hours class-based courses the Language Centre offers.

2.2. How it works: the three steps

Steps 1 and 2 are meant for autonomous learning, while Step 3 requires students to demonstrate their speaking and interacting skills to the tutor. Students receive written and oral feedback from the tutor during Steps 2 and 3.

In Step 1, before each lesson, beginners can discover and learn the fundamentals of the language through Babbel, while the advanced students learn these using a course book. All language skills are dealt with during this phase. The structure of the Babbel courses is based on a central progressive course. This course is divided into short lessons and some interesting additional courses such as culture, grammar, and idioms. The vocabulary review manager and the Babbel community serve to correct written texts. The inductive learning approach used by Babbel is based on exercises such as matching words, repeating phrases/words, filling in the blanks, listening, and completing the dialogues. Each lesson contains a clear grammar explanation where the learners can inductively discover the grammar rules. The course book I chose for the intermediate level uses a communicative and task-based approach and proposes interesting subjects to learners, providing context for real-life situations.

Step 2 helps the students to reinforce and extend what they have learnt during Step 1. I developed original training modules from scratch for speaking, listening, reading, and writing using bespoke web and task-based material. The interactive written and oral tasks I created for this phase stimulate the students to use authentic material from the internet for developing their language skills. In order to strengthen the newly-acquired vocabulary and grammar, I also developed various exercises in Quizlet. This phase is crucial for the success of the third phase, because the students can post their tasks and get my feedback, before the oral session.

The goals of the oral session are clear to students from the start of each lesson. Written tasks during Step 2 are designed for the preparation of role-plays (beginner levels) or presentations and debates (intermediate levels).

> "Naturally, the instructor must prepare the conversational tasks ahead of time so that the students know exactly what to expect and be primed with the appropriate vocabulary and grammar needed to successfully bring the task to completion" (Blake, 2016, p. 132).

However, during the oral session, the tutor proposes situations that are slightly different from the ones the students have prepared. This ensures spontaneous conversations using the learnt part of the programme.

For intermediate students, the oral test consists of two presentations delivered throughout the course, and subsequent discussion/debate with the tutor. In contrast, the beginners perform two role-plays with the tutor based on the learning material. In addition to this, all students have a written exam in order to test their listening, reading, and writing language skills. The schedule and the pace of the lessons are flexible and agreed on between tutor and student at the beginning of the course. Because the students are not allowed to miss any Skype sessions, the schedule can always be adjusted during the course in relation to changes in students' or tutors' commitments.

3. Results and discussion

The many students who followed these courses throughout the years enjoyed the very clear structure of the programme and are perfectly able to work autonomously for preparing the oral sessions. They appreciate the personal attention they get from the tutor, as well as the tailor-made extra material provided by the tutor when they feel they need extra support in a language area. Also, the flexible schedule benefits students, who often struggle to manage their busy agendas. This flexibility is also convenient for tutors who are not bound to the institutionally allocated time and places for their lessons.

Although the development of such a course requires a great deal of development time, the tutor only needs a few hours per semester to make minor adjustments, once the course structure has been set. The result is that little preparation time is required for lessons. Additionally, written feedback can be conveyed quickly using Google Docs tools. Students can also record the Skype sessions and review the feedback given in the Skype chat-box later: this has proven to be helpful for the improvement of their language skills.

Students have reported feeling satisfied with the results: the personal attention the tutor can give them helps to surface and focus on any difficulties and to offer the right support before the exam. Students' comments and suggestions allow for a continuous improvement of the programme.

The success of the web-based and interactive Italian programme led the Language Centre to extend its offering and develop a new web-based and interactive Portuguese course. Although the one-to-one lessons prove to be very effective, there is still something missing: group dynamics. Therefore, I plan to expand this course with the help of virtual reality group situations, where one-to-one lessons alternate with class sessions for virtual interaction.

4. Conclusions

Over the years, this course has proven to be a very good alternative to the traditional, face-to-face courses. These are courses that provide students with the necessary opportunities for language acquisition, and are as effective as more traditionally delivered courses. At the same time, students of all ages and in all locations, as well as those who are not enrolled at the university can participate in this course. On the tutors' side, the clear structure makes the course easy to manage. The motivation of the students in such a personalised programme ensures that the learning outcomes are high. Computer and web-based education combined with tutor expertise and feedback prove to be not only the future but also the present of the language learning process.

5. Acknowledgements

I would like to thank Christina Markanastasis and Piet C. A. Severijnen for the professional advice and inspiration I received from them.

References

Blake, R. (2016). Technology and the four skills. *Language Learning & Technology, 20*(2), 129-142. https://www.lltjournal.org/collection/col_10125_45833

Quan, Z. (2014). Motivation for a second or foreign language learning. *SHS Web of Conferences, 6*, 1-6. https://doi.org/10.1051/shsconf/20140604004

3 Do blogs as a virtual space foster students' learner autonomy? A case study

Georgie Hannam[1]

Abstract

UK higher education institutions strive to foster learner autonomy in their students to create more successful learners, yet due to its complex nature, educators and academics continue to search for effective ways to achieve this. This case study investigates how one virtual blogging space on the Independent Learning (IL) pre-sessional module at the University of Southampton seeks to cultivate learner autonomy. This qualitative study was driven by a lack of empirical research exploring both perceptions *and* practices in social learning spaces. Investigations into both of these elements help to gain a deeper understanding of how learning spaces function, which is essential to recognising how they can meet their pedagogical goals. Whilst the blogging space was effective in fostering learner autonomy to some extent, there was evidence of conflicts in how the students, IL Facilitators (ILFs), and curriculum designers perceived the blogging space. This suggests the need for more time spent conveying the rationale of the blogging space to ILFs and subsequently students, and it also highlights the wider importance of understanding individual context.

Keywords: learner autonomy, blogs, learning spaces, learner reflection, independent learning, learner strategies.

---

[1]. University of Southampton, Southampton, United Kingdom; georgie.hannam@hotmail.co.uk; https://orcid.org/0000-0003-1446-6496

How to cite this chapter: Hannam, G. (2020). Do blogs as a virtual space foster students' learner autonomy? A case study. In K. Borthwick & A. Plutino (Eds), *Education 4.0 revolution: transformative approaches to language teaching and learning, assessment and campus design* (pp. 21-27). Research-publishing.net. https://doi.org/10.14705/rpnet.2020.42.1083

Chapter 3

1. Introduction

It is widely argued that blogs increase learner autonomy by promoting active and reflective learning in an interactive learning environment (Radcliffe, Wilson, Powell, & Tibbetts, 2008; Williams & Jacobs, 2004; Chang & Yang, 2013). Murray, Fujishima, and Uzuka (2014) note that "how learners imagine a space to be, perceive it, define it, and articulate their understandings transforms a space into a place, determines what they do there, and influences their autonomy" (p. 81). This case study seeks to empirically investigate these ideas in the context of the IL module on the pre-sessional English for Academic Purposes (EAP) programme at the University of Southampton (UoS). By examining learners' perceptions and practices in the virtual blogging space, the investigation strives to determine how learners' autonomy may be affected.

2. Method

2.1. Context

The study took place on an eleven-week EAP pre-sessional programme at the UoS, focussing on the IL module which aims to support students' transition towards learner autonomy. The module supports students through weekly workshops using a flipped (blended) approach, face-to-face advisory sessions and reflective blogs, as well as various other non-compulsory activities. On the programme, it is the ILF role to run all elements of the course.

2.2. Conceptualisation of IL

IL curricular developers consider IL as "the ability to take responsibility for one's own learning" (SotonSmartSkills, 2017, p. 4), which is one of the most widely cited definitions of learner autonomy (Benson, 2013). The course designers argue that learner autonomy is achieved by learners developing their own learning strategies and subsequently being able to reflect on these. Furthermore, it involves students organising themselves, setting goals and deadlines, and evaluating their use of time and their work. IL module developers appear to hold the view that it is reflection which reinforces development and truly helps learners to progress academically (SotonSmartSkills, 2017).

2.3. Pre-sessional blogs

IL students are given a blogging topic each week and are encouraged to write a weekly blog post of two or three short paragraphs. Chang and Yang (2013) have demonstrated that blogs give students the opportunity for learners to develop reflective thought, and in the context of the pre-sessional programme the blogging topics are designed to scaffold this reflection.

The blog also serves as a safe space for students to develop their academic skills (time management, critical thinking, and research skills). Williams and Jacobs (2004) and Radcliffe et al. (2008) both recognise the importance of blogs to provide learners with a high level of autonomy whilst allowing peer-to-peer learning spaces in promoting active and reflective learning. Therefore, the course blog space is ultimately a platform which allows the ILF to support students' learning through interaction, as well as the opportunity for peer-to-peer interaction.

2.4. Methodology

This case study was heavily influenced by ethnographic research methods, allowing the investigation of social practices in their complexity rather than viewing patterns in isolation, which Dörnyei (2007) argues is one of the key principles of ethnography.

Ten students and four ILFs took part in the study. All students were of Chinese nationality in their twenties and enrolled on the UoS pre-sessional programme in preparation for their business-related Master's degrees. The ILFs had diverse professional backgrounds and a varied number of years working on the pre-sessional programme. Data was predominantly obtained from the students' blogs and semi-structured interviews, as well as from course documents (notably the

Independent Facilitator Guide – SotonSmartSkills, 2017), and observations for contextual information.

A qualitative content analysis approach (Zhang & Wildemuth, 2009) was used to analyse emerging themes to answer the research questions below.

- How do pre-sessional students and ILFs perceive, define, and articulate their understandings of the virtual blogging space?

- What social and educational practices take place in the virtual blogging space?

- To what extent does the above possibly influence students' learner autonomy practices?

3. Results and discussion

3.1. How do students and ILFs perceive, define, and articulate their understandings of the virtual blogging space?

Students and ILFs demonstrated a mismatch in how they perceived the blogs in numerous ways. Students perceived technology predominantly as a social tool, with the majority demonstrating little awareness of how it could be exploited for educational purposes. Yet, at the same time, they believed that they did not have much choice over the content of their blogs, leading students to a perceived lack of 'learner empowerment' which Little (1991) views as one of the key pillars of learner autonomy.

Furthermore, the ILFs and students demonstrated conflicting views regarding the purpose of the blogs, with many students confused about its real purpose and not contributing. Finally, there was a conflict in perceptions of the social element of blogs. Although both course developers and students expected the space to be used for student-student interaction, ILFs viewed blogs only as a space for student-ILF interaction.

3.2. What social and educational practices take place in the virtual blogging space?

The analysis found that although students did not recognise the blog to be a reflective space, almost all did engage with reflection to some extent, which is crucial to foster their learner autonomy (Little, 1991; Reinders, 2010). When evaluating the reflection, two main gaps were identified – lack of engagement with the cyclical nature of reflective processes, and reflections limited to 'surface level' rather than exploring the ideologies behind their actions.

In terms of the social interaction, not all students fully engaged with their ILFs as they did not see this as necessary, yet those that did were often more likely to develop their reflective practices on the blog further. An analysis found that responding to students with follow-up questions prompted further reflection than simply responding with statements. As well as scaffolding their learning, student-ILF interaction fostered good rapports between them which could in turn have a positive impact on learning.

Lastly, not only was the space used as a reflective tool, but the analysis also found that it served to reinforce some of the skills covered on the module, particularly critical thinking, which was determined to also be an important factor in promoting learner autonomy.

4. Conclusions

Interviews with ILFs and students showed there were some misunderstandings from both sides surrounding the intended purpose of the blogging space. In practice, ILFs were only aware of the use of blogs for teacher-student interaction, meaning that they were not promoting the virtual blogging space to its full potential.

Similarly, based on Waring and Evans' (2015, cited in SotonSmartSkills, 2017) emphasis on learners having 'voice and choice' to nurture their autonomy, course developers suggested that learners should have the freedom to direct the contents of their blog. However, possibly due to ILF instructions, participants did not perceive themselves to have this freedom. The findings of this study confirm how important the understanding of the pedagogy by teachers and/or facilitators can impact on both students' perceptions and practices as well as using such spaces to their full potential.

An analysis of the educational practices that take place in the virtual blogging space revealed that the blog does however, to some extent, influence learner autonomy practices, particularly in terms of reflection and practising other transferable study skills. This study reiterates Murray et al.'s (2014) claims that how learners perceive a space really does affect how they use the space, which in turn influences their learner autonomy. Educators should be aware of these claims in understanding how learners use their own learning spaces and how to help them in their learning journey.

5. Acknowledgements

I would like to express gratitude to my participants and colleagues on the pre-sessional programme, as well as my Master's dissertation supervisor, Vanessa Mar-Molinero.

References

Benson, P. (2013). *Teaching and researching autonomy* (2nd ed.). Taylor & Francis.
Dörnyei, Z. (2007). *Research methods in applied linguistics*. Oxford University Press.
Little, D. (1991). *Learner autonomy 1: definitions, issues and problems* (3rd ed.). Authentik.
Murray, G., Fujishima, N., & Uzuka, M. (2014). The semiotics of place: autonomy and space. In G. Murray (Ed.), *Social dimensions of autonomy in language learning* (pp. 81-99). Palgrave Macmillan. https://doi.org/10.1057/9781137290243_5

Radcliffe, D., Wilson, H., Powell, D., & Tibbetts, B. (2008). *Designing next generation places of learning: collaboration at the pedagogy-space-technology nexus.* The University of Queensland. http://citeseerx.ist.psu.edu/viewdoc/download?doi=10.1.1.215.788&rep=rep1&type=pdf

Reinders, H. (2010). Towards a classroom pedagogy for learner autonomy: a framework of independent language learning skills. *Australian Journal of Teacher Education, 35*(5), 40-54. https://doi.org/10.14221/ajte.2010v35n5.4

SotonSmartSkills. (2017). *Independent learning facilitator guide: pre-sessional programme.*

Waring, M., & Evans, C. (2015). *Understanding pedagogy: developing a critical approach to teaching and learning.* Routledge.

Williams, J., & Jacobs, J. (2004). Exploring the use of blogs as learning spaces in the higher education sector. *Australasian Journal of Educational Technology, 20*(2), 232-247. https://doi.org/10.14742/ajet.1361

Chang, Y.-S., & Yang, C. (2013). Why do we blog? From the perspectives of technology acceptance and media choice factors. *Behaviour & Information Technology, 32*(4), 371-386. https://doi.org/10.1080/0144929X.2012.656326

Zhang, Y., & Wildemuth, B. M. (2009). Qualitative analysis of content. *Analysis, 2*(1), 1-12.

4. Integrating MOOCs into traditional UK higher education: lessons learnt from MOOC-blend practitioners

Karla K. de Lima Guedes[1]

Abstract

Tertiary teaching is going through transformations as a result of web affordances, open access, and online learning platforms, such as Massive Open Online Courses (MOOCs). Some academics are taking advantage of MOOCs by integrating them into their teaching practice. This study investigates why some UK lecturers are blending MOOCs into their Face-to-Face (F2F) lecture-based teaching, how they are using them, and what they have learnt from the experience. Semi-structured interviews were conducted with six lecturers who had the experience of integrating MOOCs into their teaching. Data analysis shows that academics have a wide range of reasons for adopting this practice, with the most common reason being giving students a platform to engage in global communities and international conversations. Results generated both an understanding of why some academics are using MOOCs in their teaching practice, and a list of practical advice for MOOC-based blending novices.

Keywords: MOOCs, blended learning, higher education, open education, online learning.

---

1. University of Southampton, Southampton, United Kingdom; k.k.de-lima-guedes@soton.ac.uk; https://orcid.org/0000-0001-5470-0756

How to cite this chapter: De Lima Guedes, K. K. (2020). Integrating MOOCs into traditional UK higher education: lessons learnt from MOOC-blend practitioners. In K. Borthwick & A. Plutino (Eds), *Education 4.0 revolution: transformative approaches to language teaching and learning, assessment and campus design* (pp. 29-36). Research-publishing.net. https://doi.org/10.14705/rpnet.2020.42.1084

Chapter 4

1. Introduction

Since the creation of MOOCs, there have been discussions on their use in Higher Education (HE), in particular on how to repurpose them. A recent development in the use of MOOCs has been their integration into traditional lecture-based F2F teaching in HE (see Albó & Hernández-Leo, 2016; Fair, Harris, & León-Urrutia, 2017; Orsini-Jones, 2015; Orsini-Jones, Conde Gafaro, & Altamimi, 2017; Orsini-Jones et al., 2018; Yuan, Powell, & Olivier, 2014). However, it is still difficult to know exactly how widespread the adoption of these hybrid initiatives is and what lecturers need to take into consideration when new to this practice.

2. Method

2.1. Research setting and participants

Participants in this study were six lecturers from three UK universities who had the experience of integrating MOOCs into at least one of their F2F modules at their respective institutions (Table 1). Participants used a range of MOOCs from the FutureLearn platform. Half of the participants embedded the MOOCs into postgraduate level modules, two into undergraduate modules, and one into modules at both levels. Lecturers' levels of experience in blending MOOCs varied from blending a MOOC into their teaching for the first time to over four years of experience in designing, being in, teaching on, and blending MOOCs into F2F teaching.

Table 1. Participants' departmental affiliations and integrated MOOCs

	Affiliated department	MOOC title and platform
1	Modern Languages	Understanding Language: Learning and Teaching The Art of Teaching Foreign Languages to Young Learners Becoming a Better Teacher: Exploring Professional Development
2	Computer Science	Why We Post: The Anthropology of Social Media Learning in the Network Age
3	Archaeology	Developing Your Research Project

4	Business	The Power of Social Media
		Learning in the Network Age
		Building your Career in Tomorrow's Workplace
5	English	Jane Austen: Myth, Reality, and Global Celebrity
6	Modern Languages	English as a Medium of Instruction for Academics

2.2. Data collection and analysis

Participants were individually interviewed following a semi-structured interview. Interviews were audio recorded, transcribed, and data anonymised. The data was analysed as per thematic analysis positions of Braun and Clarke (2006, 2013) and Braun, Clarke, and Rance (2014).

3. Results and discussion

Data demonstrated that most of the lecturers believed change was taking place in HE, either in the way course content is or needed to be delivered, or on what students expected from their university experience. Results from the interviews are presented here as per Research Questions (RQs) used in the study.

3.1. RQ1: Why have lecturers decided to embed a MOOC into their F2F modules?

3.1.1. Wider discussions

The added value of taking part in wider and more global conversations was a strong theme that emerged from the interviews. All lecturers mentioned the fact that students could engage in more global conversations and explore different perspectives as one of the main reasons for the MOOC-blend. One of the most experienced lecturers strongly highlighted the importance of students' engagement in global communities, and how much students benefit from creating international connections and exploring global perspectives, which are less likely to happen in smaller localised F2F interactions.

3.1.2. Multidirectional input

Another popular theme that emerged was the possibility of students receiving input from a range of directions. Most lecturers stated that MOOCs give students the chance to hear from other experts, academics, and professionals in the area, be exposed to different voices, views, and examples, and learn from researchers who are at the top of their field.

3.1.3. Real life learning and interactions

Three of the informants stated they chose to integrate the MOOC as a way of providing students with the opportunity to learn through real life situations or interactions.

3.1.4. Digital and other transferable skills

Another reason was to add digital and transferable skills as learning outcomes to the modules. Some lecturers highlighted the importance of students developing digital skills to become more employable and aware of what pieces of technology they can use and how.

3.1.5. Additional resource

Some of the lecturers decided to use the MOOC as an additional tool to the course, to introduce topics or as a revision tool, in particular for weaker students. Most lecturers felt the content of the MOOCs was good but simplistic for university level, therefore, their content was used to introduce topics that were going to be further discussed in class.

Other themes emerged from the data, but these were only mentioned by specific lecturers. These involved students getting feedback from a wider audience, a preference for using the MOOC platform over the university's virtual learning environment, an increase in students' learning flexibility and inclusivity, and the chance to be innovative. It is important to add that all lecturers had more than one reason to integrate the MOOC into their modules.

3.2. RQ2: What suggestions did the lecturers have for new MOOC-blend practitioners?

All lecturers had pedagogical, structural, or practical changes they wanted to implement as a result of their experience, or suggestions for new MOOC-blend practitioners, and these have been divided into four categories (Figure 1).

Figure 1. Recommendations for new MOOC-based blend practitioners

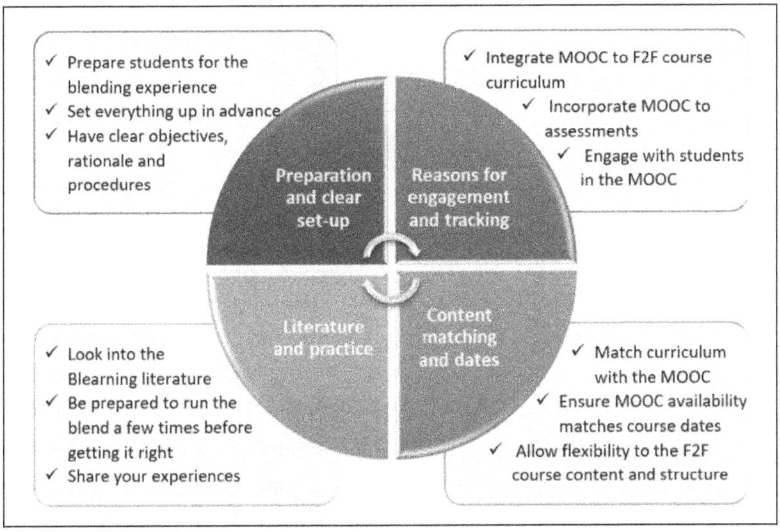

Preparation and clear set-up
- ✓ Prepare students for the blending experience
- ✓ Set everything up in advance
- ✓ Have clear objectives, rationale and procedures

Reasons for engagement and tracking
- ✓ Integrate MOOC to F2F course curriculum
- ✓ Incorporate MOOC to assessments
- ✓ Engage with students in the MOOC

Literature and practice
- ✓ Look into the Blearning literature
- ✓ Be prepared to run the blend a few times before getting it right
- ✓ Share your experiences

Content matching and dates
- ✓ Match curriculum with the MOOC
- ✓ Ensure MOOC availability matches course dates
- ✓ Allow flexibility to the F2F course content and structure

The most common advice given by the participants highlighted the importance of student preparation, course set-up, and task design. Most of the lecturers suggested having at least one session at the beginning of the F2F course to prepare students for the MOOC-blend and teach them about online learning and Netiquette. Suggestions also involved presenting the MOOC and what value it adds to students. Lecturers who had over a year of MOOC-blend experience concluded that in order to ensure students' engagement with the platform, the MOOC-based tasks needed to not only be fully integrated into the F2F course but also assessed or attached to a reward. Another suggestion given was to track students' participation, either by following and responding to them in the MOOC, or by asking students to submit their interactions as part of an assessed task.

The third category involved matching the F2F curriculum with the MOOC, and ensuring its availability matches the F2F course dates. One of the participants suggested the need to be flexible with the F2F course content and structure as matching these with the MOOC can guarantee a smoother blend.

And lastly, it was recommended that new MOOC-blend lecturers should investigate the blended learning literature and be prepared to run a few blend trials before getting it right. Data showed that more experienced MOOC-blend lecturers had tested different blending formats and that there is a need for practitioners to discuss and share their experiences due to a lack of academic publications in this area.

4. Conclusions

This paper provided an overview of some UK lecturers' drive to integrate MOOCs into their teaching and practical advice from a community of practice. Findings showed that academics have a range of reasons for adopting this practice, with the most common ones being giving students a platform to engage in global communities and international conversations and exposing them to different views and experts in the field. Results from this research provide academics with some of the initial knowledge needed prior to integrating MOOCs into F2F teaching, such as preparing students for the MOOC-blend, designing MOOC-based tasks, and matching the F2F curriculum with the MOOC content to ensure student engagement. Further discussions are needed into this practice, including its benefits, obstacles, and impact on students' learning.

5. Acknowledgements

I would like to thank Dr John Schulz and Professor Hugh Davis, my supervisors, for their guidance, and my participants for taking the time to participate in this research.

References

Albó, L., & Hernández-Leo, D. (2016). Blended learning with MOOCs: towards supporting the learning design process. *The Online, Open and Flexible Higher Education Conference, Rome, Italy, 19-21 October*. https://repositori.upf.edu/handle/10230/27478

Braun, V., & Clarke, V. (2006). Using thematic analysis in psychology. *Qualitative Research in Psychology, 3*(2), 77-101. https://doi.org/10.1191/1478088706qp063oa

Braun, V., & Clarke, V. (2013). *Successful qualitative research: a practical guide for beginners*. Sage Publications.

Braun, V., Clarke, V., & Rance, N. (2014). How to use thematic analysis with interview data. In A. Vossler & N. Moller (Eds), *The counselling & psychotherapy research handbook* (pp. 183-197). Sage Publications.

Fair, N., Harris, L., & León-Urrutia, M. (2017). Enhancing the student experience: integrating MOOCs into campus-based modules. *ICEM 2017: International Council for Education and Media, Naples, Italy, 20 -22 September*. https://eprints.soton.ac.uk/414288/

Orsini-Jones, M. (2015). *Innovative pedagogies series: Integrating a MOOC into the MA in English Language Teaching at Coventry University*. Higher Education Academy. https://www.heacademy.ac.uk/knowledge-hub/integrating-mooc-ma-english-language-teaching-coventry-university-innovation-blended

Orsini-Jones, M., Conde Gafaro, B., & Altamimi, S. (2017). Integrating a MOOC into the postgraduate ELT curriculum: reflecting on students' beliefs with a MOOC blend. In Q. Kan & S. Bax (Eds), *Beyond the language classroom: researching MOOCs and other innovations* (pp. 71-83). Research-publishing.net. https://doi.org/10.14705/rpnet.2017.mooc2016.672

Orsini-Jones, M., Conde, B., Borthwick, K., Zou, B., & Ma, W. (2018). B-MELTT: blending MOOCs for English language teacher training. *British Council ELT Research Papers*. http://teachingenglish.britishcouncil.org.cn/article/b-meltt-blending-moocs-english-language-teacher-training

Chapter 4

Yuan, L., Powell, S., & Olivier, B. (2014). *Beyond MOOCs: sustainable online learning in institutions*. CETIS. http://publications.cetis.org.uk/wp-content/uploads/2014/01/Beyond-MOOCs-Sustainable-Online-Learning-in-Institutions.pdf

5 Task-based language learning through digital storytelling in a blended learning environment

Serpil Meri-Yilan[1]

Abstract

This study investigated Task-Based Language Learning (TBLL) through Digital StoryTelling (DST) in a blended learning environment. Twenty-six Turkish university-level students prepared a DST individually and shared it with their peers in an online discussion platform. Each evaluated and graded others' DST performance based on an assessment scale. After this, they performed their stories in the classroom and similarly assessed their peer's performances. Ultimately, they were asked to give their self-reflection on the pros and cons of performing tasks online and in the classroom. Findings showed that TBLL through DST was more favoured than storytelling in the classroom and helped them to improve their speaking skills. The study suggested DST could be a positive approach in language learning and should be explored further in other language skills and multiple contexts.

Keywords: blended, digital storytelling, higher education, task-based language learning.

1. Introduction

Blended learning has come out of interest in online learning and enabled the integration of online learning with traditional learning in classrooms. With this

---

1. Agri Ibrahim Cecen University, Agri, Turkey; serpilmeri@gmail.com; https://orcid.org/0000-0003-1132-568X

How to cite this chapter: Meri-Yilan, S. (2020). Task-based language learning through digital storytelling in a blended learning environment. In K. Borthwick & A. Plutino (Eds), *Education 4.0 revolution: transformative approaches to language teaching and learning, assessment and campus design* (pp. 37-43). Research-publishing.net. https://doi.org/10.14705/rpnet.2020.42.1085

integration, TBLL can be achieved, as learners can focus on activities and tasks inside the classroom with the help of their teacher as well as outside the classroom by studying alone (Meng & Feng, 2019). Also, TBLL enables students to engage in tasks either for rewards or voluntarily for their own learning. The common definition of task in learning is regarded as an activity in which learners interact and which comprises the meaningful use of language (Bygate, 2018; Van den Branden, 2006).

Since speaking proficiency is directly proportionate to the performance of tasks, TBLL has attracted the attention of language teachers of speaking, and researchers in Second Language (SL) learning. Recent research in TBLL and speaking proficiency in online, classroom, or blended learning has indicated that:

- TBLL fosters learners' speaking proficiency because of language use in real situations and role plays (Aliakbari & Jamalvandi, 2010);

- TBLL encourages repetitiveness of tasks, which might, though, cause the neglect of learners' discussion skills (Malihah, 2010);

- TBLL motivates and engages learners with classroom learning more (Hashemifardnia, Rasooyar, & Sepehri, 2019);

- SL students as well as teachers have a more positive view on TBLL than direct tasks instruction in the classroom (Halici Page & Mede, 2018); and

- TBLL promotes learners' autonomy and self-regulated learning through teacher scaffolding (Lee, 2016).

"Task repetition" is an effective way to enhance proficiency development (Bygate, 2018, p. vi) in TBLL. Rather than performing the task repetitively, learners repeat some parts of the task instruction in a different environment, such as in a web-based environment or classroom. DST is regarded as a means to implement tasks (Lee, 2014), by which they convey "information appropriate to that particular task to another person" (Cook, 2008, p. 257). However, there has been little research investigating TBLL through DST, especially in the area of face-to-face storytelling compared to online storytelling.

2. Method

2.1. Participants

The present study was conducted as a follow up to a previous one (Meri Yilan, 2020), which looked into students engaged with performing a task through DST. Results showed that participants had a positive view on DST, so the author decided to investigate it further by adding TBLL through DST, which will be analysed in this paper.

Twenty-six students from a Turkish state university (21 females and five males) participated in the present study, which was made a compulsory part of their speaking course. All participants had intermediate English levels, as determined by their course test, and they had previously engaged with performing a task through DST.

2.2. Implementing TBLL through DST in a blended learning environment

Considering their familiarity with DST, a task was given to each of them based on Ribeiro's (2015) proposal for an integrated approach to DST: story circle, creation, and show. First, all of them were asked to prepare a mini seminar about either the importance of sport, a place for holiday, the advantages of living in a city, or the perfect job. Before this task, they were lectured about how to prepare and perform a mini seminar. Next, they were told to record either their video or both video and audio and post their recording on a class in Google Classroom created by their lecturer. By this, every student could see their peers' performances. After that, they were reminded to evaluate others' performance according to an assessment scale given by the lecturer (i.e. introducing the topic, organising ideas, using expressions, and giving examples to points) and post their grade under the performance. Finally, they performed their seminar in the classroom in front of their lecturer and peers. In the meantime, each assessed and graded others' performances according to the scale and handed in their assessment of both performances to their lecturer.

2.3. Data collection instruments and analysis

Data were collected from self-reflection reports on their performance in both virtual and physical classrooms in April and May 2019. Students expressed their opinions on their feelings about DST and in-classroom storytelling. Data from each view were categorised under 'only pros', 'only cons', and 'both pros and cons', and analysed using Excel 2016.

3. Results and discussion

Data showed that students had different views on TBLL through DST in the blended learning environment, comparing their performance in virtual and physical classrooms. Nearly all of them found TBLL through storytelling in the virtual environment more advantageous than in the classroom (see Figure 1 and Figure 2), as consistent with the study by Halici Page and Mede (2018). Data also indicated that Ribeiro's (2015) approach to DST is effective in improving speaking proficiency if students are familiar with DST.

Figure 1 presents that 24 students stated that DST was easier and effective as they were able to rehearse their performance in a comfortable way before recording their video and audio, and improved their speaking and autonomous learning, as they evaluated their speaking. However, one student found it difficult to both record and perform the task at the same time. Likewise, another student mentioned the difficulty in recording when performing but stated that she was happy since no one was around her.

Figure 2 indicates that 22 students noted that they found TBLL in the physical classroom more disadvantageous in that they were worried, anxious, and excited to perform it in front of the crowd. Notwithstanding its cons, ten of them expressed that they needed this kind of TBLL in order to prove themselves in every way of speaking English. Furthermore, two of them wrote that TBLL in the physical environment was effective to overcome their nervousness and improve themselves. Additionally, two of them thought that they had both positive and negative experiences in the physical TBLL environment in that they were very excited at first but were relaxed when they started performing the task.

All in all, this study shows that students felt that they improved their learning, especially speaking, due to the lower anxiety levels in the blended learning environment, corroborating studies by Aliakbari and Jamalvandi (2010) and Bygate (2018), and TBLL, particularly in the virtual environment, fostered learner autonomy in line with the study by Lee (2016).

Figure 1. Students' views on TBLL in Google Classroom

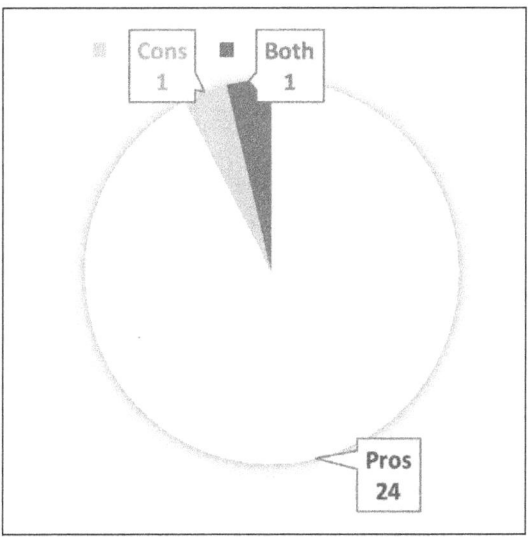

Figure 2. Students' views on TBLL in the classroom

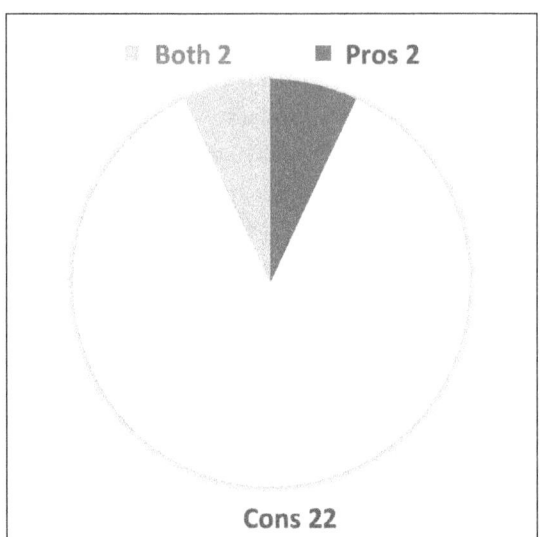

4. Conclusions

This research showed that DST can be used as a means to diminish shyness and has a positive impact on students' speaking proficiency. However, it does not work alone to overcome their excitement, anxiety, and worry in the classroom. This study suggests that a well-designed collaborative learning activity through DST can be effective to promote learning. Further studies could develop our understanding of DST between different nationalities and countries in terms of other language skills or learning.

References

Aliakbari, M., & Jamalvandi, B. (2010). The impact of 'role play' on fostering EFL learners' speaking ability: a task-based approach. *Journal of Pan-Pacific Association of Applied Linguistics, 14*(1), 15-29.

Bygate, M. (2018). (Ed.). *Learning language through task repetition*. John Benjamins Publishing Company.

Cook, V. (2008). *Second language learning and language teaching*. Hodder Education.

Halici Page, M., & Mede, E. (2018). Comparing task-based instruction and traditional instruction on task engagement and vocabulary development in secondary language education. *The Journal of Educational Research, 111*(3), 371-381. https://doi.org/10.10 80/00220671.2017.1391163

Hashemifardnia, A., Rasooyar, H., & Sepehri, M. (2019). Enhancing Iranian EFL learners' speaking fluency through using task-based activities. *Global Journal of Foreign Language Teaching, 9*(1), 024-032. https://doi.org/10.18844/gjflt.v9i1.3998

Lee, L. (2014). Digital news stories: building language learners' content knowledge and speaking skills. *Foreign Language Annals, 47*(2), 338-356. https://doi.org/10.1111/flan.12084

Lee, L. (2016). Autonomous learning through task-based instruction in fully online language courses. *Language Learning & Technology, 20*(2), 81-97.

Malihah, N. (2010). The effectiveness of speaking instruction through task-based language teaching. *Register Journal, 3*(1), 85-101. https://doi.org/10.18326/rgt.v3i1.1152

Meng, F., & Feng, C. (2019). Task-based language teaching for EFL students based on blended learning. In *2019 4th International Conference on Humanities Science and Society Development (ICHSSD 2019)*. Atlantis Press. https://doi.org/10.2991/ichssd-19.2019.28

Meri Yilan, S. (2020). Promoting cultural awareness through digital storytelling in higher education. In F. Nami (Ed.), *Digital storytelling in second and foreign language teaching* (pp. 203-228). Peter Lang Publishing. https://doi.org/10.3726/b15897

Ribeiro, S. (2015). Digital storytelling: an integrated approach to language learning for the 21st century student. *Teaching English with Technology, 15*(2), 39-53.

Van den Branden, K. (2006). *Task-based language teaching: from theory to practice*. Cambridge University Press.

6 Introducing corpus linguistic tools to EFL undergraduates and trainee teachers

Mária Adorján[1]

Abstract

Many language teachers use Information and Communications Technology (ICT) in their classrooms to create tasks, quizzes, or polls with general online learning platforms. Few teachers have experience, however, of incorporating online corpus tools in their teaching or assessment practices. This paper will explore how autonomous learning can be fostered by gradually introducing freely available lexical databases, online collocation dictionaries, pronunciation guides, concordancers, N-gram extractors, and other text analysis tools for vocabulary building, skills practice, or self-checking. Tasks used with English as a Foreign Language (EFL) undergraduates and teacher trainees on a Master's Teaching English as a Foreign Language (MA TEFL) course will be presented. I will also explain why having some familiarity with linguistics research can enable teachers to use these applications more meaningfully.

Keywords: corpus linguistic tools, EFL, vocabulary learning, text analysis, language teacher training.

---

1. Károli Gáspár University of the Reformed Church, Budapest, Hungary; adorjan.maria@kre.hu; https://orcid.org/0000-0001-8870-3947

How to cite this chapter: Adorján, M. (2020). Introducing corpus linguistic tools to EFL undergraduates and trainee teachers. In K. Borthwick & A. Plutino (Eds), *Education 4.0 revolution: transformative approaches to language teaching and learning, assessment and campus design* (pp. 45-51). Research-publishing.net. https://doi.org/10.14705/rpnet.2020.42.1086

Chapter 6

1. Introduction

Teachers are increasingly aware of online tools that can support the teaching of EFL and are willing to incorporate a large number of them into their courses in higher education. These tools are used for many purposes, from supporting individual work to networking or sharing content. The use of online language reference tools based on corpus data is still in its infancy, though, both in English language teaching and in teacher training (Granath, 2009). At Karoli Gaspar University, EFL undergraduates and trainee teachers are offered a range of courses where corpus linguistic tools and techniques are used regularly, including study skills, advanced writing, business English, and a dedicated course for students on the MA TEFL module: Foreign Language Assessment Methods.

Advanced level language learners have specific needs that make them distinct from other learners. Learning languages at higher levels necessitates different learning strategies than learning at beginners' levels (Politzer & McGroarty, 1985). The main differences lie in vocabulary acquisition and production: having learnt most words within the core vocabulary range (the first 2,000 word-families), they have to acquire words within a lower frequency band (Nation, 2006). This requires a more conscious effort on the learners' part to actively look for opportunities to learn more words, or read much more in order to facilitate incidental learning (Schmitt, 2000). If students are informed about word frequency lists, or other applications based on corpus linguistics, they can easily optimise their learning processes. Another advanced learner problem is finding the right collocations. A concordancer can help to produce multi-word expressions used by native speakers or competent L2 users. Students also need to be aware of diverse discourse characteristics to sound natural or appropriate in various communicative environments. Samples of these, again, are difficult to find in coursebooks.

Corpus linguistics research can help in the above areas by raising awareness, speeding up the learning process, and promoting learner autonomy (Gavioli, 2009). In language teaching and learning, three main types of corpora are studied most often: authentic corpora to observe language use (Szudarski, 2017), learner corpora to study interlanguage (Granger, 2002), and multilingual corpora for translation studies and contrastive analysis (Flowerdew, 2012). The aim of this paper is to present a variety of corpus linguistic tools based on these three types of corpora, which were incorporated into the syllabi of several university courses for EFL learners.

2. Method

The use of online tools was first incorporated into several language courses in 2018, as early as in the first semester. Table 1 lists some of these tools with their functions and their online location, however this paper will only discuss the first two in detail. In the first term, students were trained by demonstrating how each tool worked, explaining research findings which related to the tool, and by encouraging students to experiment with real data (their own texts, for instance); also, to compare their findings with research results. The use of corpus tools had two main aims: to facilitate the self-assessment of work, and to help students improve their writing and speaking skills. From the second year onwards, the main focus was analysing authentic original and translated texts and textbook language.

Students assessed their work in two main areas: receptive vocabulary knowledge and text production. The first tool they used was Vocabulary Profiler (lextutor.ca), which was used to analyse essays to find the ratio of academic words. Next, they compared their results with authentic text characteristics provided in the Typical Profiles section. The Vocabulary Size Test revealed the differences among students in their passive word knowledge. Doing the test stimulated a discussion on language learning styles and strategies, and discussing the results provided an opportunity to become familiar with some research into optimal vocabulary size for various purposes (Nation, 2006).

The process of using the tools to check individual texts went through these phases: drafting the text, familiarisation with the tool (e.g. what vocabulary levels exist, how to check words with the tool), analysing the text with the tool (e.g. types of vocabulary used, the ratio of K1, K2, and academic words), reflecting on, analysing, and peer-discussing the results, then finally, rewriting the text and submitting it.

Table 1. The functions of corpus tools with the website

Tool name	Function	Link to website
Lextutor Vocabulary Profiler	textual analysis for vocabulary levels (K1, K2, ... AWL)	https://www.lextutor.ca/vp/eng/
Vocabulary Size Test	testing receptive vocabulary knowledge, multiple choice format	https://my.vocabularysize.com/ or https://www.lextutor.ca/tests/
Cambridge English Dictionary	monolingual word search; checking CEFR[2] levels of word senses	https://dictionary.cambridge.org/dictionary/english/
Vocabulary Kitchen	CEFR level visualiser for texts	http://vocabkitchen.com/profiler/cefr
Coh-Metrix	cohesion and text readability analysis	http://tea.cohmetrix.com/
Oxford Collocation Dictionary (free version)	how words are used together in a sentence	http://www.ozdic.com/
Sketch Engine for Language Learners	concordance, exploring immediate context of words	https://skell.sketchengine.eu/#home?lang=en
Google Books N-Gram Viewer	historical use of words or expressions	https://books.google.com/ngrams
Wordnet Editor	finding and visualising words and synonym sets; differentiating word senses	http://wordventure.eti.pg.gda.pl/wne/wne.html
Multidimensional Analyser	six features characteristic of various genres (Biber, 1992)	https://sites.google.com/site/multidimensionaltagger/home

3. Results and discussion

Introducing corpus linguistic tools into various EFL courses resulted in an overall positive outcome, based on end-of-term student feedback[3]. During the

---

2. Common European Framework of Reference for languages

3. End-of-term course evaluation forms, unpublished raw data.

sessions, students were provided with numerous practice opportunities so that they knew the rationale behind the tools' use in teaching, and felt comfortable experimenting with them at home. With such scaffolding provided (Hubbard, 2013), corpus linguistic tools have become an essential part of the syllabus without an explicit focus on applied linguistics research. The students, according to their feedback, gained empirical evidence about the quality of their writing and were able to assess themselves, thus creating an atmosphere of involvement, interaction, individualisation, and independence (terminology from Dudley-Evans & St John, 1998, p. 200).

The heavily technology-enhanced L2 environment meant, however, that there were some anxiety issues at the start of the course that had to be overcome. Even though all students are surrounded daily by ICT, individual help was necessary for those who were new to monitoring language, focussing on syntax, or understanding grammatical terminology. Another important consideration is that for the successful use of corpus linguistic tools in such courses, the language teacher needs to be literate in corpus linguistic research so that results can be connected to existing corpus findings and language acquisition theories.

4. Conclusions

The use of corpus linguistic tools in a variety of courses at the university had not been considered previously: it emerged rather as a response to EFL learners' needs. The rationale behind introducing these tools was to raise language awareness and enable learner autonomy. The students' direct exposure to corpus linguistic tools occurred without offering an introductory course into the field. An active search to incorporate additional tools followed this phase, when it became clear that the students were motivated and involved in the explorations.

An important conclusion to be drawn from the end-of-term assessment of the courses was that scaffolding was essential twice: at the students' first attempts with the tools and when they wanted to interpret the results. This latter was essential particularly in the case of tools which only provided numerical data as results. These percentages and ratios lent themselves to discussion, and the teacher could direct the group to further readings about the features of the language analysed.

I hope that sharing these ideas will provide the language teaching community with potential corpus linguistic activities, and the widespread use of these tools will have a significant impact on traditional higher education language courses.

5. Acknowledgements

I would like to thank my students who let me use their work for textual analysis.

References

Biber, D. (1992). On the complexity of discourse complexity: a multidimensional analysis. *Discourse Processes, 15*(2), 133-163. https://doi.org/10.1080/01638539209544806

Dudley-Evans, T., & St John, M. J. (1998). *Developments in ESP. A multidisciplinary approach.* Cambridge University Press.

Flowerdew, L. (2012). Definitions, purposes and applications of corpora. In L. Flowerdew (Ed.), *Corpora and language education* (pp. 3-35). Palgrave Macmillan. https://doi.org/10.1057/9780230355569_1

Gavioli, L. (2009). Corpus analysis and the achievement of learner autonomy in interaction. In L. Lombardo (Ed.), *Using corpora to learn about language and discourse* (pp. 39-69). Peter Lang.

Granath, S. (2009). Who benefits from learning how to use corpora? In K. Aijmer (Ed.), *Corpora and language teaching* (pp. 47-65). John Benjamins Publishing.

Granger, S. (2002). A bird's-eye view of learner corpus research. In S. Granger, J. Hung & S. Petch-Tyson (Eds), *Computer learner corpora, second language acquisition, and foreign language teaching* (vol. 6, pp. 3-33). John Benjamins Publishing.

Hubbard, P. (2013). Making a case for learner training in technology enhanced language learning environments. *Calico Journal, 30*(2), 163-178. https://doi.org/10.11139/cj.30.2.163-178

Nation, P. (2006). How large a vocabulary is needed for reading and listening? *Canadian Modern Language Review, 63*(1), 59-82. https://doi.org/10.3138/cmlr.63.1.59

Politzer, R. L., & McGroarty, M. (1985). An exploratory study of learning behaviors and their relationship to gains in linguistic and communicative competence. *Tesol Quarterly, 19*(1), 103-123. https://doi.org/10.2307/3586774

Schmitt, N. (2000). *Vocabulary in language teaching.* Cambridge University Press.

Szudarski, P. (2017). *Corpus linguistics for vocabulary: a guide for research.* Routledge.

7 EAP 4.0: Transforming the English for Academic Purposes Toolkit to meet the evolving needs and expectations of digital students

Andrew Davey[1] and Simone Marx[2]

Abstract

The English for Academic Purposes (EAP) Toolkit provides a wide range of online learning resources which are used in a mixture of self-study, blended, and classroom settings, primarily by students whose first language is not English. The Toolkit was developed by the eLanguages team at the University of Southampton and first licensed in 2004. This paper describes the most recent major refreshment project to improve both the functionality and appearance of the Toolkit. With the latest updates, we have aimed to increase the appeal of the resources to encourage greater autonomous usage by students, and to improve the ease with which staff can recommend and use Toolkit resources with their students. In this paper we introduce the key updates to the resources, including new functionalities and features, expanding the Toolkit with additional learning resources, a new visual approach, responsive feedback, accessibility upgrades, and strategies for increasing student usage.

Keywords: EAP, blended learning, self-study, English, TEL.

---

1. University of Southampton, Southampton, United Kingdom; a.davey@soton.ac.uk; https://orcid.org/0000-0002-0007-462X

2. University of Southampton, Southampton, United Kingdom; s.marx@soton.ac.uk

How to cite this chapter: Davey, A., & Marx, S. (2020). EAP 4.0: Transforming the English for Academic Purposes Toolkit to meet the evolving needs and expectations of digital students. In K. Borthwick & A. Plutino (Eds), *Education 4.0 revolution: transformative approaches to language teaching and learning, assessment and campus design* (pp. 53-59). Research-publishing.net. https://doi.org/10.14705/rpnet.2020.42.1087

Chapter 7

1. Introduction

The EAP Toolkit (eLanguages, 2020a) is a set of interactive online learning resources for students whose first language is not English. The Toolkit was first launched in 2004 and has been licensed by a range of institutions within the UK and internationally.

The Toolkit consists of materials in the form of Learning Objects (LOs), which may be used as standalone resources or as part of a structured course (Polsani, 2003). The LOs are suitable for students' self-study and for blended use within a classroom.

The purpose of the transformation project, the most ambitious refreshment since 2014, is to enhance the usefulness of the resources in the following five ways, each of which will be detailed in this article:

- expanding the range of resources available in the Toolkit;

- improving the accessibility of the resources within the Toolkit, including adding captions to audio and video materials;

- providing structured learning for students and tutors using the Toolkit;

- producing publicity materials to encourage students and tutors to use the Toolkit at licensing institutions; and

- improving the 'look and feel' of the Toolkit.

Since the Toolkit was first licensed in 2004, digital learning has become more widely used by institutions. Alongside this, students have come to expect more from their digital resources. As such, it was important to refresh the Toolkit in line with wider web design progression to ensure that the resource remains relevant and enjoyable for students to use.

2. Expanding the range

The EAP Toolkit started with 86 LOs in 2004 and was expanded to 100 in 2007. A further expansion to 114 LOs took place in 2011. Since 2011, a number of institutions have taken out institutional licences to use the Toolkit with native speakers of English as well as those with a different first language. As a result, it was felt that broadening the range and depth of resources by integrating some from the Study Skills Toolkit (produced in the same format as the EAP Toolkit but aimed at native English speakers) would be a way to adapt the Toolkit to suit how it is being used. This has expanded the resource set to 130 LOs.

3. Accessibility

To improve the accessibility of the Toolkit and bring all aspects in line with the Public Sector Accessibility Regulations, it was important to implement captions for all audio clips (Legislation.gov.uk, 2018). To achieve this, transcripts were created alongside audio timings. These were constructed into a video text track file for each clip.

To both improve the accessibility of the LOs and add variety to existing resources, it is planned that existing videos will be re-recorded alongside a provision of new videos. All videos will be recorded with clear visibility of speakers' mouths to enable users to lip-read, with captions provided alongside (see Figure 1). These provisions not only improve the accessibility of the Toolkit for users with hearing impairments, they also augment the overall usability of the resources provided.

Figure 1. An example audio clip with accompanying captions

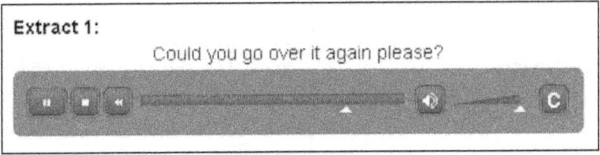

4. Structured learning

The EAP Toolkit has traditionally had a simple, hierarchical structure. Each of the LOs was categorised into one of seven folders, depending on its core skill area. It was felt that, with the expansion of the resource set, this linear approach could be enhanced by providing additional routes and directions for students and tutors on how to make best use of the resources.

Prepare for Success (eLanguages, 2020b; Watson, 2009), an online pre-arrival course for international students, has a set of guided routes through the resources on the website called 'Study Pathways'. This course was developed using a similar learning object model, by the same team. It was felt that this model would be a good concept to adapt for the EAP Toolkit, allowing users to choose LOs according to which skill or topic they hope to improve. We implemented a 'tags and pathways' approach to organising LOs in the Toolkit, as this was felt to be an accessible means of organising resources. In order to implement this 'tags and pathways' approach, each LO was assigned a number of keywords, and the 15 most frequently occurring keywords became tags directing users to the corresponding LOs (see Figure 2). With this refreshed structure it is hoped that users will be able to optimise their learning by choosing to complete LOs which are specifically relevant to their own learning needs.

Figure 2. Icons for the new pathways and tags feature

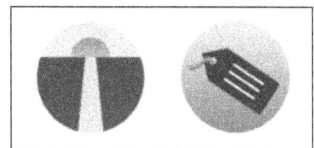

5. Publicity

Several institutions have struggled to find ways to engage students in using the EAP Toolkit for self-study. As a consequence, it was decided that an internal promotion pack would help institutions to be able to increase student usage. The pack consists of templates for posters and bookmarks which can be customised and used to direct students towards the Toolkit. There are also suggested study uses in the pack, to encourage tutors to use the resources for specific purposes in a blended context in the classroom (see Figure 3).

Figure 3. Example of a customised internal publicity poster

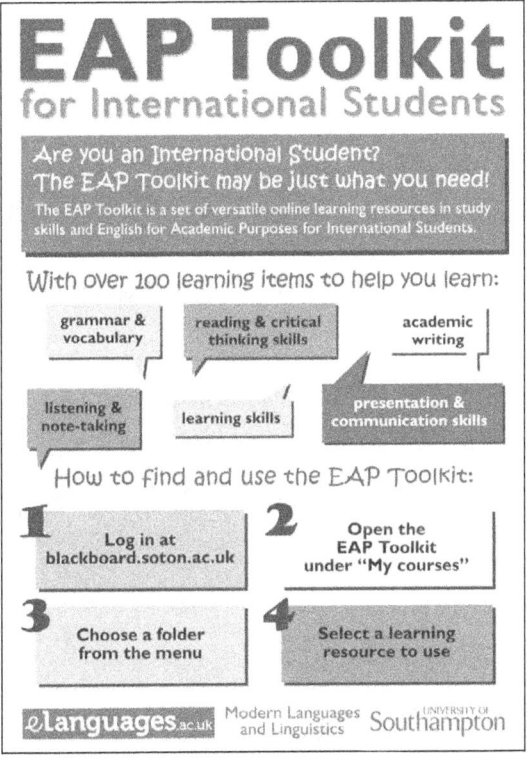

6. Look and feel

It was important to update the appearance of the EAP Toolkit to make it more modern-looking and improve the existing mobile experience for users. As a result, the Toolkit's style was updated to present an up-to-date, sleek, and engaging style. As part of this, a cohesive colour scheme was implemented across the Toolkit to facilitate a joined-up user experience. The structure of LOs was also updated to improve their appearance and usability on mobile devices. To ensure these updates were appropriate for a wide range of devices, the Toolkit underwent thorough testing across a variety of devices and browsers, including Android and iOS phones and tablets, as well as Chrome, Safari, Opera, Firefox, and Edge. The style was further updated through the implementation of the aforementioned 'tags and pathways' system, which improves the organisation of LOs and enables users to select activities based on the skills and themes particularly relevant to each individual.

A significant element of the update was the redesigning of the Toolkit's icons. Key to this was the implementation of a cohesive colour scheme alongside simple yet modern icons. Following the rough outline and drafting of possible ideas, the icons were designed in Adobe Photoshop (see Figure 4).

Figure 4. The six updated icons representing weblinks, instructions, dictionaries, feedback, summaries and the glossary (left to right)

7. Conclusions

Since the Toolkit's last major refreshment in 2014, approaches to web design have evolved significantly. As a result, these stylistic changes warranted updating the Toolkit's look and feel to make it more in keeping with these developments. Added to this, it was important to ensure the content remained current.

Although these updates are in the preliminary stages of implementation, it is felt that, with the completion of this refreshment project, the EAP Toolkit's usability and appeal to both students and staff will be enhanced. With the increased number of resources provided, the refreshed style and structure of the Toolkit will enable students to navigate the range of resources with greater ease to address specific topics and skills requiring improvement. In turn, with the addition of captions for all audio and video clips, the Toolkit will become more appealing and accessible to users. Ultimately, these updates enhance users' experiences of the Toolkit, facilitating more targeted, effective, and enjoyable digital learning.

References

eLanguages. (2020a). *English for academic purposes toolkit*. https://www.elanguages.ac.uk/eap_toolkit.php

eLanguages. (2020b). *Prepare for success*. https://www.prepareforsuccess.org.uk/

Legislation.gov.uk. (2018). *The public sector bodies (website and mobile applications) accessibility regulations*. https://www.legislation.gov.uk/uksi/2018/852/contents/made

Polsani, P. (2003). Use and abuse of reusable learning objects. *Journal of Digital Information, 3*(4). https://journals.tdl.org/jodi/index.php/jodi/article/view/89/88

Watson, J. (2009). Prepare for success: a pre-arrival learning resource to prepare students for study in different academic culture. *Conference Paper, EUNIS 2009*.

8 Chinese parents' perceptions and practices of EFL technology usage with young children

Xing Liu[1]

Abstract

Despite a large body of literature on the Technology Acceptance Model (TAM), studies on young children's usage of media technology in China are still scant. This paper characterises the variations in Chinese parental acceptance and intent to continue related to their children's use of web-based English as a Foreign Language (EFL) technologies. A sample of 20 parents from an inland city in China participated in individual interviews and reported factors affecting their acceptance and preferences. Thematic analysis reveals that parents' beliefs about EFL affect the perceived ease of use and perceived usefulness of EFL technologies. The study has also found that Chinese parents are now attaching more importance to children's emotional and social skills development.

Keywords: TAM, EFL, e-learning, parents.

1. Introduction

Despite a large body of literature on the TAM (Davis, 1989), studies on young children in China are still scant (Bittman, Rutherford, Brown, & Unsworth, 2011; Lieberman, Bates, & So, 2009; Lieberman, Fisk, & Biely, 2009; Plowman, McPake, & Stephen, 2010).

---

1. North Minzu University, Yinchuan, Ningxia, China; liuxing@nun.edu.cn; https://orcid.org/0000-0003-0969-3483

How to cite this chapter: Liu, X. (2020). Chinese parents' perceptions and practices of EFL technology usage with young children. In K. Borthwick & A. Plutino (Eds), *Education 4.0 revolution: transformative approaches to language teaching and learning, assessment and campus design* (pp. 61-67). Research-publishing.net. https://doi.org/10.14705/rpnet.2020.42.1088

Davis (1989) proposed the TAM to understand factors affecting user behaviour. The TAM implies that people's acceptance and rejection of technology is influenced by their cognition and belief. It suggests that the Perceived Ease Of Use (PEOU) and Perceived Usefulness (PU) are two core factors in explaining user attitudes towards using, behavioural intentions, and actual use. Figure 1 shows the interplay among TAM elements. Although TAM has been validated in various technology contexts (e.g. e-commerce, Wu & Wang, 2005) and regions (e.g. Taiwan, Tsuei & Hsu, 2019), researchers pointed out that this model lacks explanatory power because it does not clearly define external variables (Legris, Ingham, & Collerette, 2003). In other words, what factors affect PEOU and PU? Specifically, this paper tries to identify the external variables that affect parents' perceptions and in turn their practices.

Figure 1. A common operationalisation of the TAM (adapted from Davis, 1989)

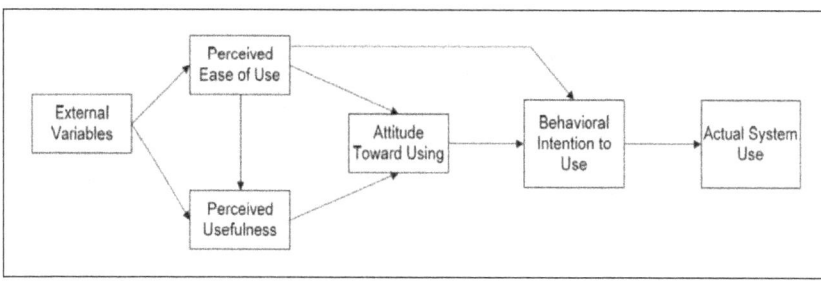

Plowman and McPake (2013) looked into how parents might have the greatest influence on children's early developmental stages. Parental perceptions and practices either directly or indirectly relate to children's technology habits and behaviours, for example, concerning technology access (e.g. whether or not to buy an iPad, amount of screen time), function (e.g. for family time or education), attitudes (e.g. health concerns), and support (e.g. emotional or technical help), etc.

This paper attempts to explore factors that influence parental perceptions and beliefs using the TAM. The findings will provide a better understanding of how Chinese parents' prior EFL experiences and beliefs influence their PEOU and PU of EFL apps and whether cultural and social specific factors exist in technology acceptance studies.

2. Method

This study was set in Y city, a small and less developed northwest inland city in China. While previous studies about children's technology use in China were largely conducted in more prosperous metropolitan cities in coastal or eastern areas, such as Beijing, Shanghai, and Shenzhen, the relatively lower-middle socio-economic level of Y city fills the literature gap by providing a different context since a body of literature has shown a strong relationship between parents' socio-economic status, parenting styles, and children's technology use (Gjelaj, Buza, Shatri, & Zabeli, 2020; Liu, Georgiou, & Manolitsis, 2018; Zhu et al., 2019).

Parents in this study were from a local mid-tier kindergarten. Tuition fee is the major criteria when the tier a kindergarten belongs to is decided. In total, 20 parents (17 mothers, three fathers) were recruited and participated in the study. Their ages ranged from 29 to 39 years and their children's ages ranged from 3-6. All of them have used EFL technology in the past year.

Parents responded individually to an exploratory 20-minute semi-structured interview to elicit the maximum depth of their attitudes and perceptions. Some questions included were as below.

- What types of EFL mobile devices do you have at home?
- Why do you let your child use this EFL App?
- What is your expectation of using this EFL App?

A thematic analysis (Braun & Clarke, 2006) was then conducted and interviews were transcribed and then coded by the researcher using the software Nvivo 12.

3. Results and discussion

Two major sub-themes emerged as the most important factors contributing to either acceptance or rejection of an EFL app: parents' EFL beliefs, as well as their parenting goals.

3.1. Parents' EFL beliefs

Language related beliefs are most mentioned when parents answered the question of why or not they use particular apps. Most of the parents mentioned in their interviews their EFL beliefs and how these beliefs direct their practices. Many parents responded to the question of 'why use' by ascribing great value to English. For example, they claimed that the reason for using the app is

> "English is useful. If you want to travel abroad by yourself, you have to learn English. At least you need to learn some daily communication vocabulary".

But some parents expressed their doubts about the importance of English, either because of the advent of modern translations technologies or because of the heightened status of Chinese. They said

> "I don't want my daughter to spend too much time on English. China is becoming more powerful and perhaps when my daughter grows old, the world will all speak Chinese".

Apart from language ideologies, parents also indicated that they thought there was a 'critical period' for English learning (Penfield & Roberts, 1959), i.e. when learning a foreign language is easier and thus they claimed 'the earlier, the better' and made the following statement:

> "undoubtedly, the earlier, the better, especially when you consider pronunciation. If you let your child learn English at a very early age, he could speak like a native".

3.2. Parenting goals

Nearly all parents mentioned parenting goals in their interviews as an explanation for technology acceptance, rejection, or abandonment. However, it is interesting that these beliefs are inconsistent and sometimes contradictory.

Table 1 below shows results of the thematic analysis. A classification and illustration of the patterns about goals and specific expectations as well as the signifiers (what represents the goals) display the variety of parental expectations and their relationship with technology acceptance. Parents who place great emphasis on children's academic achievement, especially on test scores, show high regard for using EFL apps, while parents who prioritise social and emotional development express concerns with children's use of EFL apps. It is also interesting that some academic achievement-orientated parents also worry that use of apps may reduce children's classroom attention level due to the relatively more entertaining features of modern technology.

Table 1. Parenting goals and EFL technology acceptance

Parental Goals	Parental Expectation	Signifiers	Technology Acceptance	Technology Rejection
Academic	Emphasis on learning outcome	test scores	14	6
	Emphasis on learning process	classroom attention	8	12
Social	Communicative skills	understanding classroom rules	7	13
Emotional	Emotional welfare	loneliness, courage, and other emotional issues	7	13

4. Conclusions

This paper provides insights into parent's acceptances and intentions for continued use of young children's EFL apps. The study found that parents' prior EFL beliefs and parenting goals have a strong impact on both initial use and continued use. Parents with a more optimistic view towards Chinese language are more likely to reject or abandon EFL apps, while parents who are more concerned with children's test scores show more willingness to adopt an EFL app.

These findings also provide further insights into how external factors rather than the app itself affect people's technology acceptance. However, the limited number of participants calls for further investigations, especially a qualitative one to confirm these findings. It should also be stressed that since this study was conducted in a small inland city in China, results may differ should it be replicated in other regions, due to the presence of a vast socio-economic gap.

References

Bittman, M., Rutherford, L., Brown, J., & Unsworth, L. (2011). Digital natives? New and old media and children's OlitCOmeS. *Australian Journal of Education*, *55*(2), 161-175. https://doi.org/10.1177/000494411105500206

Braun, V., & Clarke, V. (2006). Using thematic analysis in psychology. *Qualitative research in psychology*, *3*(2), 77-101. https://doi.org/10.1191/1478088706qp063oa

Davis, F. D. (1989). Perceived usefulness, perceived ease of use, and user acceptance of information technology. *MIS Quarterly: Management Information Systems*, *13*(3), 319-339. https://doi.org/10.2307/249008

Gjelaj, M., Buza, K., Shatri, K., & Zabeli, N. (2020). Digital technologies in early childhood: attitudes and practices of parents and teachers in Kosovo. *International Journal of Instruction*, *13*(1), 165-184. https://doi.org/10.29333/iji.2020.13111a

Legris, P., Ingham, J., & Collerette, P. (2003). Why do people use information technology? A critical review of the technology acceptance model. *Information & management*, *40*(3), 191-204. https://doi.org/10.1016/s0378-7206(01)00143-4

Lieberman, D. A., Bates, C. H., & So, J. (2009). Young children's learning with digital media. *Computers in the Schools*, *26*(4), 271-283. https://doi.org/10.1080/07380560903360194

Lieberman, D. A., Fisk, M. C., & Biely, E. (2009). Digital games for young children ages three to six: from research to design. *Computers in the Schools*, *26*(4), 299-313. https://doi.org/10.1080/07380560903360178

Liu, C., Georgiou, G. K., & Manolitsis, G. (2018). Modeling the relationships of parents' expectations, family's SES, and home literacy environment with emergent literacy skills and word reading in Chinese. *Early Childhood Research Quarterly, 43*(November), 1-10. https://doi.org/10.1016/j.ecresq.2017.11.001

Penfield, W., & Roberts, L. (1959). *Speech and brain mechanisms.* Princeton University Press.

Plowman, L., & McPake, J. (2013). Seven myths about young children and technology. *Childhood Education, 89*(1), 27-33. https://doi.org/10.1080/00094056.2013.757490

Plowman, L., McPake, J., & Stephen, C. (2010). The technologisation of childhood? Young children and technology in the home. *Children and Society, 24*(1), 63-74. https://doi.org/10.1111/j.1099-0860.2008.00180.x

Tsuei, M., & Hsu, Y. Y. (2019). Parents' acceptance of participation in the integration of technology into children's instruction. *Asia-Pacific Education Researcher, 28*(5), 457-467. https://doi.org/10.1007/s40299-019-00447-3

Wu, J. H., & Wang, S. C. (2005). What drives mobile commerce? An empirical evaluation of the revised technology acceptance model. *Information and Management, 42*(5), 719-729. https://doi.org/10.1016/j.im.2004.07.001

Zhu, S., Yang, H. H., Macleod, J., Shi, Y., & Wu, D. (2019). Parents' and students' attitudes toward tablet integration in schools. *International Review of Research in Open and Distributed Learning, 19*(4). https://doi.org/10.19173/irrodl.v19i4.2970

Author index

A
Adorján, Mária v, 2, 45

B
Borthwick, Kate iv, 1

C
Capitani, Laura v, 2, 15

D
Davey, Andrew v, 3, 53
De Lima Guedes, Karla K. v, 2, 29

G
Goria, Cecilia vi, 1, 5
Guetta, Lea vi, 2, 5

H
Hannam, Georgie vi, 2, 21

L
Liu, Xing vi, 3, 61

M
Marx, Simone vi, 3, 53
Meri-Yilan, Serpil vi, 2, 37

P
Plutino, Alessia iv, 1

www.ingramcontent.com/pod-product-compliance
Lightning Source LLC
Chambersburg PA
CBHW031638160426
43196CB00006B/473